SPORTS

TAE KWON DO

by Mari Schuh

AMICUS | AMICUS INK

uniform

belt

Look for these words and pictures as you read.

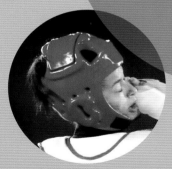

helmet

trunk pad

Kick! Punch! Block!
It's tae kwon do!

A match begins.
It lasts three rounds.
The athlete with the
most points will win.

Do you see the uniform?

It is called a dobok.

It is usually white.

uniform

Do you see the belts?
The colors show the rank.
The best rank is black.

belts

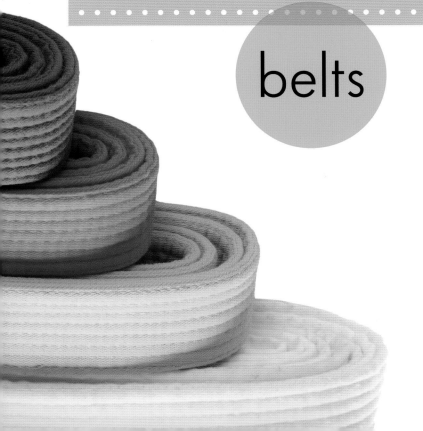

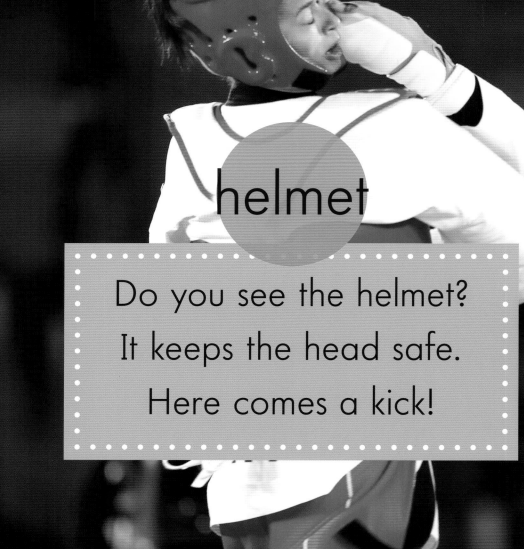

helmet

Do you see the helmet?
It keeps the head safe.
Here comes a kick!

Do you see the trunk pad?
Sensors in it feel
when it gets hit.

trunk pad

Look at the kick! The foot hits the chest. Two points!

uniform

belts

Did you find?

helmet

trunk pad

Spot is published by Amicus and Amicus Ink
P.O. Box 1329, Mankato, MN 56002
www.amicuspublishing.us

Library of Congress Cataloging-in-Publication Data
Names: Schuh, Mari C., 1975- author.
Title: Tae kwon do / by Mari Schuh.
Description: Mankato, MN : Amicus, [2020] |
Series: Spot sports | Audience: K to Grade 3.
Identifiers: LCCN 2018037393 (print) | LCCN 2018053231
   (ebook) | ISBN 9781681517360 (pdf) | ISBN 9781681516547
   (library binding) | ISBN 9781681524405(pbk.)
Subjects: LCSH: Tae kwon do--Juvenile literature. | Picture
   puzzles--Juvenile literature.
Classification: LCC GV1114.9 (ebook) | LCC GV1114.9 .S35
   2020 (print) | DDC 796.815/7--dc23
LC record available at https://lccn.loc.gov/2018037393

Printed in China

HC 10 9 8 7 6 5 4 3 2 1
PB 10 9 8 7 6 5 4 3 2 1

For Isaac and Dan Ruemping
—MS and JQ

Wendy Dieker, editor
Deb Miner, series designer
Aubrey Harper, book designer
Holly Young, photo researcher

Photos by Gerville/iStock cover,
16; Lucian Coman/Shutterstock
1; Andrew Medichini/AP 3;
Ministério da Defesa, Sgt Johnson
Barros/WikiCommons 4–5;
bokan76/iStock 6–7; Dole08/
iStock 8–9; David Davies/PA
Wire/AP 10–11; Glow Asia RF/
Alamy 12–13; Canadian Press
Photos/AP 14–15

TAE KWON DO